THE CHALLENGE OF SAMUKAI!

TITAN
COMICS

LEGO® GRAPHIC NOVELS
AVAILABLE FROM TITAN™

NINJAGO #1 (3 Oct 14)

NINJAGO #2 (3 Oct 14)

NINJAGO #3 (7 Nov 14)

NINJAGO #4 (7 Nov 14)

NINJAGO #5 (5 Dec 14)

NINJAGO #6 (5 Dec 14)

NINJAGO #7 (2 Jan 15)

NINJAGO #8 (2 Jan 15)

NINJAGO #9 (6 Feb 15)

TITAN COMICS

#1 THE CHALLENGE OF SAMUKAI!

GREG FARSHTEY • Writer
PAULO HENRIQUE • Artist
LAURIE E. SMITH • Colorist

TITAN
COMICS

LEGO® NINJAGO™ Masters of Spinjitzu
Volume One: The Challenge of Samukai!

Greg Farshtey – Writer
Paulo Henrique – Artist
Laurie E. Smith – Colourist
Bryan Senka – Letterer

Published by Titan Comics, a division of Titan Publishing Group Ltd., 144 Southwark St., London, SE1 0UP. Contains material originally published in single comic form as LEGO NINJAGO: VOLUME #1: THE CHALLENGE OF SAMUKAI! LEGO, the LEGO logo and Ninjago are trademarks of the LEGO Group ©2014 The LEGO Group. All rights reserved. All characters, events and institutions depicted herein are fictional. Any similarity between any of the names, characters, persons, events and/or institutions in this publication to actual names, characters, and persons, whether living or dead and/or institutions are unintended and purely coincidental. License contact for Europe: Blue Ocean Entertainment AG, Germany.

A CIP catalogue record for this title is available from the British Library.

Printed in China.

First published in the USA and Canada in March 2012 by Papercutz.

10 9 8 7 6 5 4 3 2 1

ISBN: 9781782761921

www.titan-comics.com

www.LEGO.com

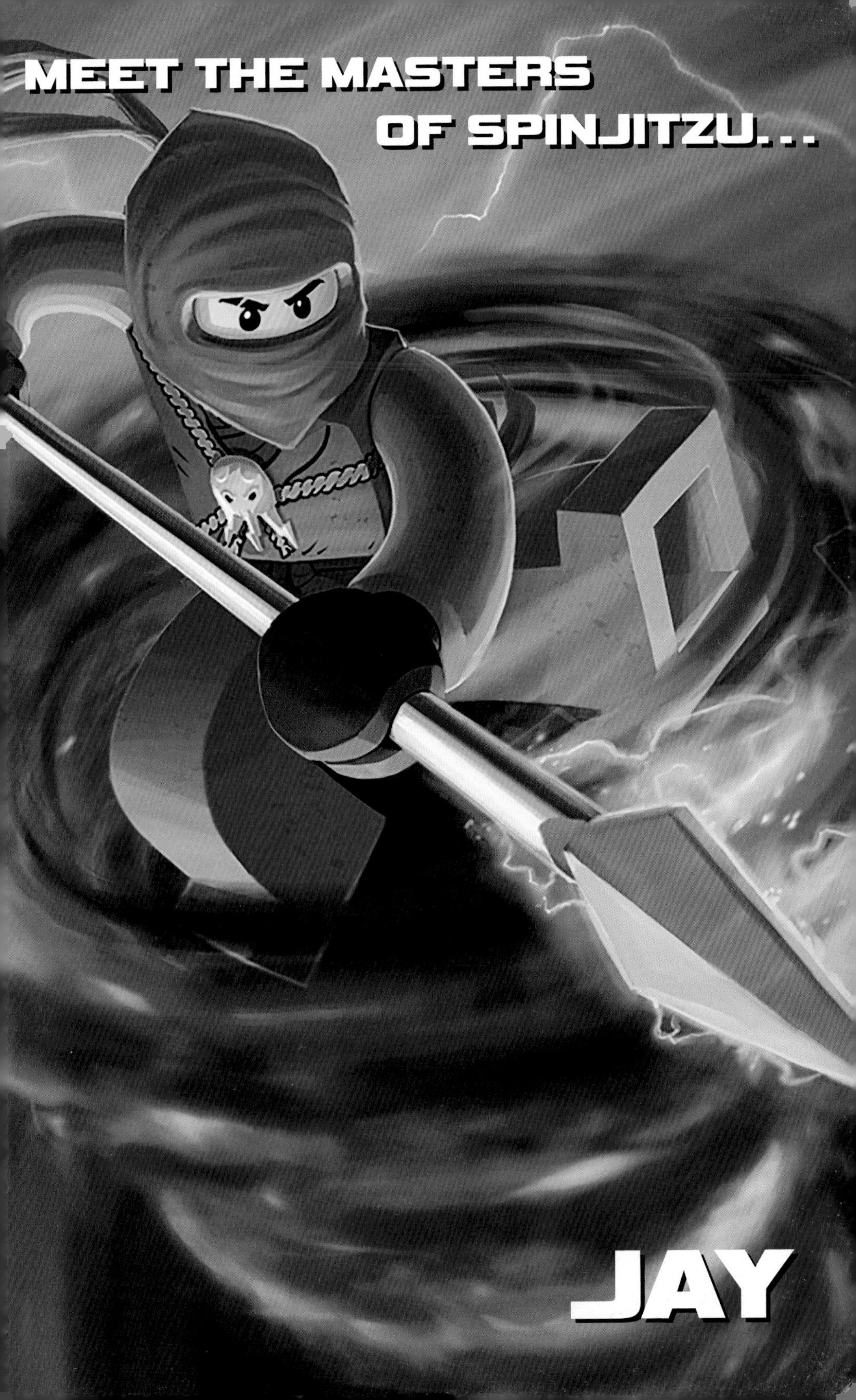
MEET THE MASTERS
OF SPINJITZU...
JAY

COLE

ZANE

KAI

NYA

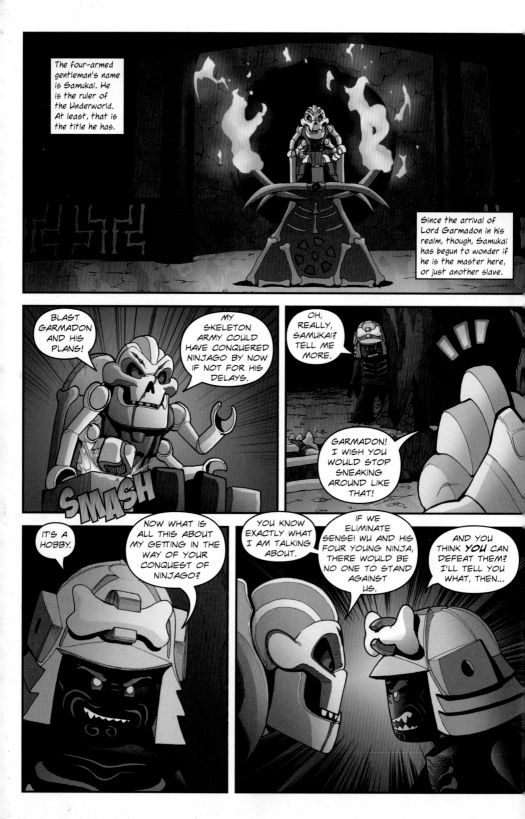

LET'S MAKE A BET.

THE WAGER,
PART ONE

GREG FARSHTEY -- HONORABLE WRITER
PAULO HENRIQUE -- AUGUST ARTIST
LAURIE E. SMITH -- HUMBLE COLORIST
BRYAN SENKA -- LOYAL LETTERER
MICHAEL PETRANEK -- EDITORIAL STUDENT
JIM SALICRUP -- EDITORIAL MASTER

ORIGINS

Gamblin' Greg Farshtey — Writer • Poker-faced Paulo Henrique — Artist

Laurie "Let-it-ride" E. Smith — Colorist • Bettin' Bryan Senka — Letterer

Michael "The Player" Petranek — Associate Editor • Jim "Jackpot" Salicrup — Editor-in-Chief

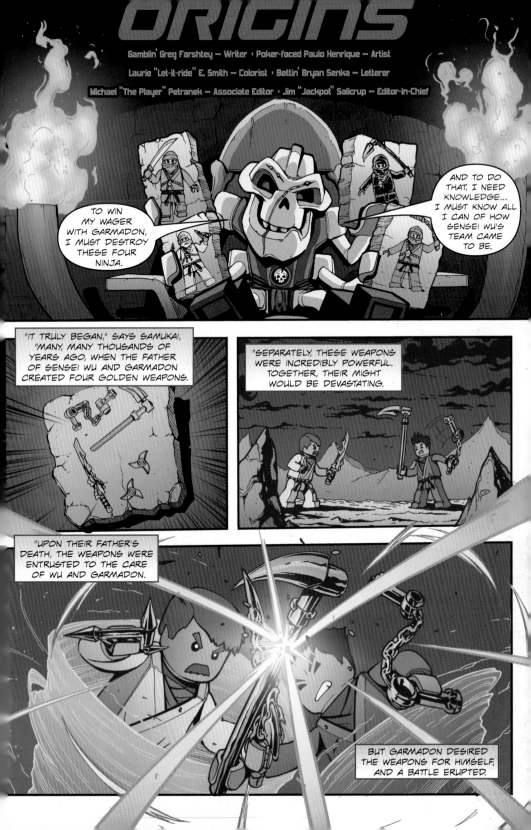

TO WIN MY WAGER WITH GARMADON, I MUST DESTROY THESE FOUR NINJA.

AND TO DO THAT, I NEED KNOWLEDGE... I MUST KNOW ALL I CAN OF HOW SENSEI WU'S TEAM CAME TO BE.

"IT TRULY BEGAN," SAYS SAMUKAI, "MANY, MANY THOUSANDS OF YEARS AGO, WHEN THE FATHER OF SENSEI WU AND GARMADON CREATED FOUR GOLDEN WEAPONS.

"SEPARATELY, THESE WEAPONS WERE INCREDIBLY POWERFUL. TOGETHER, THEIR MIGHT WOULD BE DEVASTATING.

"UPON THEIR FATHER'S DEATH, THE WEAPONS WERE ENTRUSTED TO THE CARE OF WU AND GARMADON.

BUT GARMADON DESIRED THE WEAPONS FOR HIMSELF, AND A BATTLE ERUPTED.

"THE FUTURE SENSEI WU WAS THE VICTOR, AND GARMADON WAS BANISHED TO THE UNDERWORLD... MY REALM. IT SEEMED THAT THE GOLDEN WEAPONS WERE SAFE FOREVER.

"SENSEI WU HID THE WEAPONS AWAY. USING THE POWER OF SPINJITZU, HE FOUGHT FOR 'JUSTICE' THROUGHOUT THE LAND AND BECAME A HERO TO THOSE IDIOTIC MORTALS ON THE WORLD OF NINJAGO.

"STILL, HE NEVER RELAXED HIS GUARD. HE KNEW THE FOUR WEAPONS OF SPINJITZU HAD TO BE PROTECTED. AND ONE DAY, AS HE REACHED OUT ACROSS THE PLANET WITH HIS SENSES, HE SUDDENLY KNEW...

"GARMADON HAD RETURNED!

"THE SENSEI'S EVIL BROTHER HAD ALLIED WITH ME AND PLANNED TO USE MY SKELETON ARMY TO STEAL THE FOUR WEAPONS AND CONQUER NINJAGO. THE INVASION HAD ALREADY BEGUN!

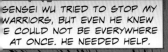

SENSEI WU TRIED TO STOP MY WARRIORS, BUT EVEN HE KNEW E COULD NOT BE EVERYWHERE AT ONCE. HE NEEDED HELP.

"HE SET OUT TO RECRUIT A TEAM OF YOUNG MEN HE COULD TRAIN AS NINJA, FROM THE TOP OF THE HIGHEST PEAK..."

A GREAT EVIL STALKS THIS LAND, COLE...

"TO THE BOTTOM OF A FROZEN LAKE..."

IF MY BROTHER SEIZES CONTROL OF THE FOUR WEAPONS OF SPINJITZU, OUR WORLD IS DOOMED, ZANE...

"AND EVERYWHERE IN BETWEEN."

THAT IS WHY I NEED YOUR HELP, JAY. WILL YOU AID ME?

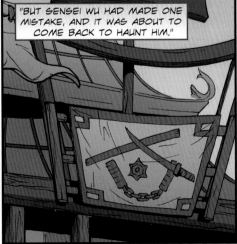

"BUT SENSEI WU HAD MADE ONE MISTAKE, AND IT WAS ABOUT TO COME BACK TO HAUNT HIM."

"BUT KAI WASN'T HARMED. IN FACT, HE FOUGHT WELL. BUT WHILE HE WAS BATTLING SOME OF MY WARRIORS--"

"THE OTHERS WERE TAKING WHAT WE HAD REALLY COME THERE FOR: KAI'S SISTER AND A LITTLE SOMETHING THAT WAS, UNKNOWN TO THEM, CONCEALED INSIDE THE BANNER OF THEIR SHOP!"

HELP! KAI!

RIPPPPP

"IT WAS ONLY LATER THAT SENSEI WU WOULD TELL KAI JUST WHY WE HAD ATTACKED THAT LITTLE VILLAGE."

LONG AGO, I ASKED YOUR FATHER TO MAKE A MAP FOR ME, SHOWING WHERE THE FOUR WEAPONS OF SPINJITZU WERE HIDDEN.

THAT MAP WAS CONCEALED IN THE HWEAPONS BANNER-- AND NOW GARMADON AND HIS SKELETON ALLIES HAVE IT.

TO SAVE YOUR SISTER, YOU NEED TRAINING.

JOIN MY TEAM-- BECOME A NINJA-- AND TOGETHER, WE WILL STOP GARMADON AND SAVE NYA.

I DON'T CARE ABOUT ANY OF THAT. I WANT MY SISTER BACK!

ARE YOU GOING TO HELP ME FIND HER, OR DO I DO IT ON MY OWN?

"KAI'S FINAL TEST WAS TO BATTLE JAY, COLE, AND ZANE, SENSEI WU'S THREE NINJA.

"TO FAIL AGAINST THESE THREE WOULD ROB KAI OF ANY CHANCE OF RESCUING HIS SISTER.

"BUT HE DID NOT FAIL. NOW HE FIGHTS ALONGSIDE THE OTHER THREE, WHO HAVE BECOME HIS BEST FRIENDS. TOGETHER, THEY DARE TO ATTEMPT TO STOP GARMADON'S MASTER PLAN."

Not far from the temporary campsite of Sensei Wu and his four ninja...

OKAY, SO, WHEN I SEE KAI, I CHASE AFTER HIM.

NO, NUCKAL, YOU LET HIM CHASE AFTER YOU.

RIGHT, GENERAL KRUNCHA, BUT NO MATTER WHAT, DON'T LET HIM NEAR THE CRYSTAL CAVES.

NO, YOU NUMBSKULL, YOU WANT HIM TO GO INTO THE CRYSTAL CAVES! YOU'RE SUPPOSED TO LEAD HIM THERE!

HOW I'M SUPPOSED TO TRAP A NINJA WITH HELP LIKE THIS, I DON'T--

YOU WERE WRONG, GENERAL. MY SKULL'S NOT NUMB. I SURE FELT THAT!

WHACK

TURN ABOUT

"GORILLA" GREG FARSHTEY -- WRITER
"PILEDRIVER" PAULO HENRIQUE -- ARTIST
"LOCK 'N' LOAD" LAURIE E. SMITH -- COLORIST
"BAD BOY" BRYAN SENKA -- LETTERER
"MAD DOG" MICHAEL PETRANEK -- ASSOCIATE EDITOR
"JAWBREAKER" JIM SALICRUP -- EDITOR-IN-CHIEF

I'M SO DONE... AGAIN. ALL RIGHT, NUCKAL, LET'S GO OVER IT ONE MORE TIME.

28

GREG FARSHTEY -- WRITER * PAULO HENRIQUE -- ARTIST * LAURIE E. SMITH -- COLORIST *
BRYAN SENKA -- LETTERER * MICHAEL PETRANEK -- ASSOCIATE EDITOR * JIM SALICRUP -- EDITOR-IN-CHIEF

39

FORTUNATELY, WHEN YOU KNOW SPINJITZU, FALLING ISN'T SO SCARY.

MY TURNADO SLOWS MY FALL AND HERE I AM, ACROSS THE RIVER. WONDER WHAT SURPRISE WAITS FOR ME HERE?

OH. THAT SURPRISE.

What Cole could not know, as he met his new challenge, was that Samukai's spies had informed him of all that was taking place.

SO, THE YOUNG NINJA HAS TO MAKE CHOICES? THEN LET'S GIVE HIM ONE.

Samukai arranged an ambush, capturing Kai and Jay as bait for a trap for Cole.

The credits caption reads:

GREG (THE MASTERMIND) FARSHTEY -- WRITER • PAULO (THE ENFORCER) HENRIQUE -- ARTIST
LAURIE E. (THE BAIT) SMITH -- COLORIST • BRYAN (THE GO-BETWEEN) SENKA -- LETTERER
MICHAEL (THE NEGOTIATOR) PETRANEK -- ASSOCIATE EDITOR • JIM (THE PATSY) SALICRUP -- EDITOR-IN-CHIEF

The battle was quick.

Caught by surprise, the skeletons have no time to defend themselves.

Seemingly everywhere at once, four ninja might as well be 400.

Although some of the skeletons also know spinjitzu, they cannot match the skill of Zane and the rest.

It didn't take long for Samukai to see how the fight was going to end...

THE FOOLS MAY TURN MY WARRIORS INTO A BONEYARD, BUT THEY WON'T CATCH ME.

THE WAGER,
PART TWO

GREG FARSHTEY -- WISEST WRITER
PAULO HENRIQUE -- ABSOLUTE ARTIST
LAURIE E. SMITH -- CONSUMMATE COLORIST
BRYAN SENKA -- LEARNED LETTERER
MICHAEL PETRANEK -- ACCOMPLISHED ASSOCIATE EDITOR
JIM SALICRUP -- ECCENTRIC EDITOR-IN-CHIEF

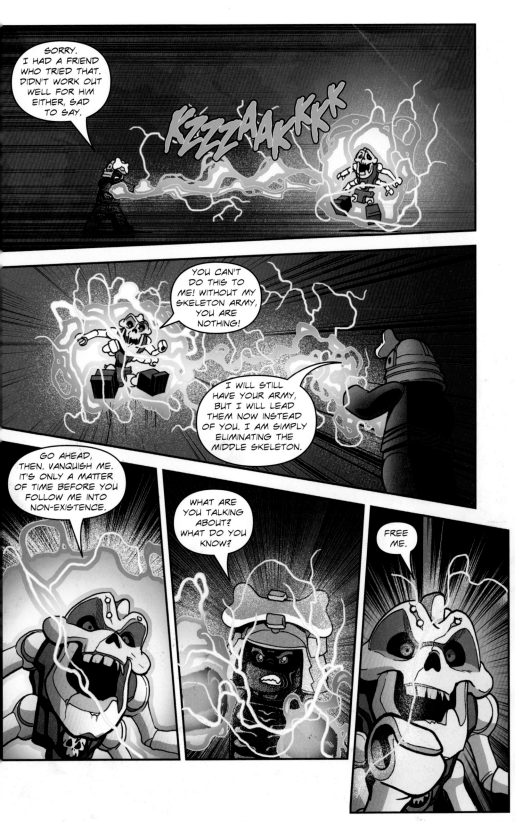

VERY WELL.

UNNNGH!

KKRRAASSHH

I KNOW THE RULES OF THE UNDERWORLD. YOU DON'T.

WHY DO YOU THINK I HAVE NEVER ATTEMPTED TO BETRAY YOU?

BECAUSE I KNOW YOUR TIME HERE WILL BE OVER SOON, ONE WAY OR THE OTHER.

IN YOUR SHADOW FORM, YOU CAN ONLY EXIST FOR SO LONG.

YOUR OWN WILL HAS KEPT YOU "ALIVE" ALL THESE YEARS, BUT EVEN YOU CAN ONLY RESIST THE NATURE OF THIS PLACE FOR SO LONG.

YOU'RE LYING...

YOU NEED THE GOLDEN WEAPONS, AND THE POWER THEY CONTAIN, SOON -- OR YOU WILL CEASE TO BE EVEN A SHADOW.

I AND MY SKELETON WARRIORS CAN GET THEM FOR YOU. BUT WITHOUT ME, MY ARMY WILL FALL APART AND BE USELESS.

I MADE YOU A WAGER, AND I WON.

NOW YOU SAY I WILL BE GAMBLING MY EXISTENCE IF I TRY TO COLLECT WHAT I AM OWED--

A MOST INTERESTING PROBLEM.

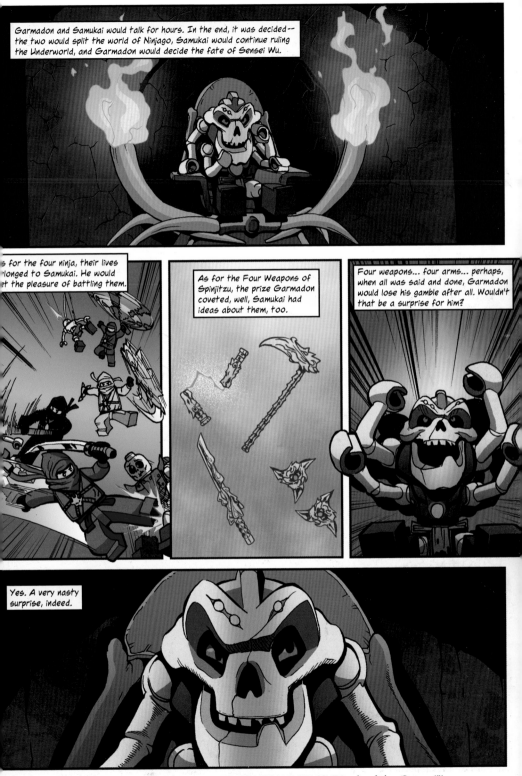

Garmadon and Samukai would talk for hours. In the end, it was decided-- the two would split the world of Ninjago, Samukai would continue ruling the Underworld, and Garmadon would decide the fate of Sensei Wu.

...s for the four ninja, their lives ...longed to Samukai. He would ...t the pleasure of battling them.

As for the Four Weapons of Spinjitzu, the prize Garmadon coveted, well, Samukai had ideas about them, too.

Four weapons... four arms... perhaps, when all was said and done, Garmadon would lose his gamble after all. Wouldn't that be a surprise for him?

Yes. A very nasty surprise, indeed.

The Four Ninja Will Return in LEGO® NINJAGO™ #2 "Mask of the Sensei"!

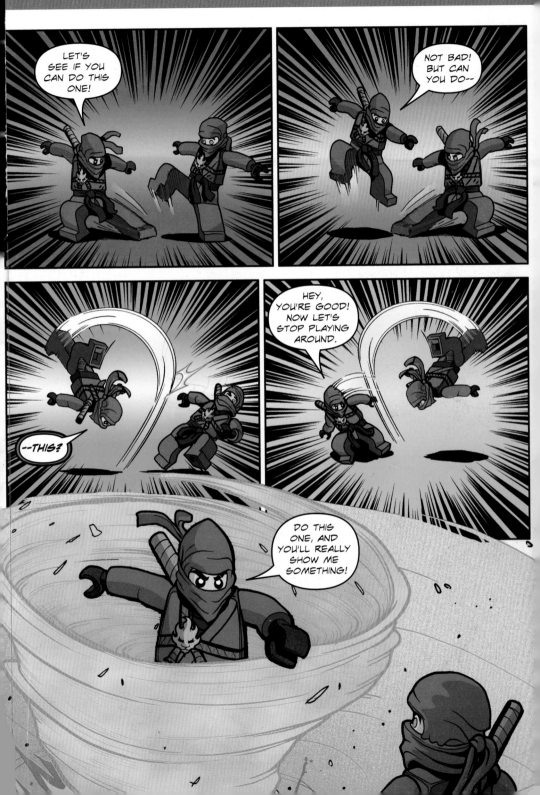

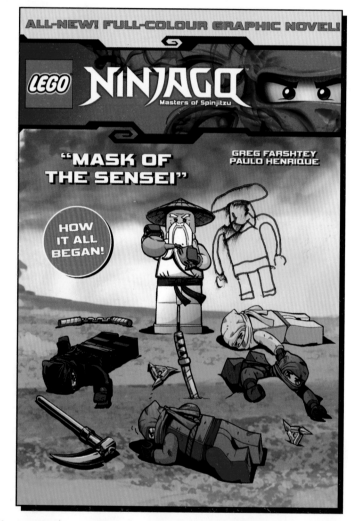